LOVE IS ALL I NEED

GAURAV MALHOTRA

LOVE STORIES & EMOTIONS IN POETIC FORMAT

DK's Books For All

Delhi

Published by
D K's Books For All
A-6, Nimri Commercial Centre,
Ashok Vihar Phase-IV,
Delhi 110052
Phones: +91 11 27302453
e-mail: info@Lppindia.com
website: www.Lppindia.com

First Published 2009

ISBN-10: 81-7386-275-3
ISBN-13: 978-81-7386-275-5

Printed at
D K Fine Art Press P Ltd.
Delhi 110052

PRINTED IN INDIA

Dear Friends,

Just before you give a look at what lies ahead of you in this book, I would like to share some words with you.

'LOVE' is a feel that we all cherish. It brings us happiness though at times along with pain. Still no matter be the age, we all desire it and long for it.

To win or to loose is not the point. The phase, during which we experience it, is the most precious of all. Just having gone through this phase makes us stand stronger and somewhere in our eyes we see ourselves as more fortunate. Now all my friends, who haven't experienced it yet, don't loose heart, as it's just a matter of time, when it hits you across.

"Love Is All I Need" is my attempt to present in front of you a collection of situations, thoughts & feelings that has been experienced & felt, with time by the mankind; in the form of poetry backed up with some fictional stories. So, with no exception, you may find its resemblance in your life or in your thoughts too.

Now finally, before you turn the page, lets just say 'CHEERS' together, simply in the name of 'LOVE'.

GAURAV MALHOTRA
Email: gmalhotra@live.com.sg

Our sincere thanks to

McDowell's No.1

BRIGHT
OUTDOOR MEDIA PVT. LTD.

Contents

SECTION - IX

SECTION - I

NOW THAT YOU ARE GONE

Prologue

(There are times in our life when we feel deserted or cheated. So, as the name suggests 'NOW THAT YOU ARE GONE', is all about the feelings of a man deserted by his lady love. This man now can neither accept the fact nor is able to regain his senses. So in the middle of the night he walks up to her and speaks his heart out.)

Now that you are gone,
I feel completely shattered.
We sang for so long,
But suddenly lost, what mattered.

A look in your eyes,
Made me accomplish unexpected heights.
Now that my heart cries,
I have lost my urge to fight.

You were my strength, you were my power.
Now that you are gone, I am getting drowned in this shower.
I know I need to rise, but nothing seems wise.
For without you life is too much of a price.

How come you turned so mean, and left me behind,
With only memories on my mind, which I need to rewind.
This cannot be the end, for its not the way we liked.
Rise back, my Love! Or take me by your side.

IMMORTAL PACT

Prologue

(The most common aspect among lovers is once finding themselves ill-fated, they usually turn to alcohol assuming it would relieve them of their pain. Here is a similar guy who after loosing his love is unable to return to his senses and has turned completely alcoholic; drinking day & night. Though one day, on his way home being drunk, he discovers that he is no longer alone in this world and finally finds solace to his heart, thereafter declining alcohol forever and leading his life in a constructive way. Well 'IMMORTAL PACT' is a look in his unique discovery of finding solace.)

Here, with all the clouds above,
Saw the moon, riding dove.
Walking across, a misty lane,
Came a girl, down from plane.

With the night, so silent & so dark,
She touched my heart, with a spark.
Then she kissed, my lips so hard,
I was taken, off my guard.

Her eyes shined blue, as our gaze, stuck glue.
She struck as flu, and I had no clue.
The time fly by, and I didn't ask why.
Why should I, for she was, my.

I hold her tight, for I had the right.
To my surprise, she turned to light.
Next moment, she walked away.
"Please, don't go", was all I could say.

"I am always yours", was her reply,
"O my Love! Please don't cry".
She smiled at me, and I smiled her back,
For our love is an immortal pact.

CRUSH

Prologue

(Remember the first time when just seeing a face or a look in eyes made your heart slip, as if it never belonged to you. That rush of blood, that desire to posses leading you to a dreamy state. Right, 'CRUSH', as the name itself suggests, is something sweet & light. It did or does happen with us all, so let's see how it makes this guy fall.)

Lying on the bed, with my eyes closed,
I didn't realise, when I dozed.
Came a butterfly, and sat by my side,
Caressed me gently, and took me on a ride.

We walked along the mountains; we walked along the sands,
Holding together, each others hand.
Suddenly I woke up, and looked outside the window,
I saw a girl, who was playing bingo.

She was the same, as the one in dream,
Stuck my breath, as I was about to scream.
Down I rushed, opened the door,
And moved out, towards the group of four.

Reaching up near, I stopped by side,
As she looked up, with her eyes open wide.
Fall her cards, and I helped her pick,
She said, "Thanks", and my heart clicked.

We stood still, as moments passed,
Till her friends, shook us apart.
Her eyes were smiling, and so were mine,
She just blushed, while my heart shined.

Now that she has come, into my life,
She is the one, to be my wife.
Don't know its love, or just crush,
But in the process, I forgot to brush.

A MOMENT TO REMEMBER

Prologue

(No matter what be the age, one always remembers the first time, the first night shared with their love. The way we came close, the impulse that made us break all barriers, the innocence that was guided by desire and then the next morning which made us realize that now it's time to part, bringing us a pain mixed with pleasure, the pleasure of oneness; no doubt it's a moment we can never forget and will cherish forever. 'A MOMENT TO REMEMBER' is simply a replica of that state.)

Here comes the sun,
And blemishes the beauty of night.
She will have to leave,
And won't be there in my sight.

She will be gone soon,
But her fragrance be all around.
With her in my arms,
I feel like owing million pounds.

The smoothness of her skin,
And the way she handles,
Makes me feel like,
The wax of burning candles.
Her passionate eyes,
And the shade from her hair,
Blooms my soul,
As if lit by chandeliers.

The warmness of her bosom,
And the sweetness of her lips,
Plunges my heart,
As my pulse rate dips.

So please, O Sun Lord!
Go back to your hiding,
And you, my dear moon,
Just keep on riding.

Let me hold her close,
For a moment or two long.
And let the world come still,
As if, it's a never ending song.

SECTION - II

ON THE MOUNTAIN TOP

EVERY TIME YOU COME RAINBOW APPEARS

Prologue

(Well let me tell you a story. There lived a guy at countryside. Tall, robust, fair & handsome, with long hairs; his name was James. With a love for nature and big dreams in his eyes, a passionate guy he was. Queen of his heart was a girl named Tina, having freshness of a breeze and as charming as the moon.

They had been close pals since childhood, but now in their late teens the heat reached the point where it was bound to get ignited. Hence this evening when Tina has come to meet James on a mountain top, James pops up the question saying, 'EVERY TIME YOU COME RAINBOW APPEARS'.)

Every time you come rainbow appears,
Enlightening my life full of tears.
Are you an angel or just another girl?
For me you are precious, as precious as pearl.

The seven colours of rainbow,
Are shades of your personality.
No, I ain't a flatterer,
I can prove the factuality.
The desire of rainbow acts as stimulus,
For ensuring the sun to emerge out of clouds.
Then finally he feels happy, eventually also proud,
When is being thanked by those on the ground.

Now may I put up a question I always wanted to?
Answer it genuinely if you really do.
Look sun has existence and rainbow is occurrence,
Can occurrence turn existence just for our preference?

LONELY

After listening to what James said on the mountain top, all Tina did say was that she herself felt the same. Their joys knew no bounds, they embraced each other and stayed there close looking at the sunset as time flew along and came up the stars. But before departing James assured Tina of one thing that no matter be the odds, he will rise high in his life and all he wanted from her, was to stay by his side.

(Unfortunately, in spite of all his hardships the lady luck eluded James. All his efforts to rise for some or other reasons ended up with the same result; all flops. Then one night Tina met him again on the mountain top and said she was planning to get married and it wasn't him. James was so grief struck & shocked that he couldn't utter a word and just watched Tina walking away, with his wet eyes. He stayed there for hours with storms blowing hard in his mind. And after hours of gustiness, he found his mind finally at calm, with complete silence all around. Being at ease now, he gets up, picks his jacket and 'LONELY' walks towards his home with heavy feet in the early hours of morning.)

Lonely I lie,
Lonely I cry,
Lonely I make my ways,
Through what my heart says.
Lonely I stand,
Lonely I fall,
Lonely I fight,
With my head held tall.

Me lonely, is all that matter.
Let the world do, all its chatter.

The belief in me, will overcome, the irony of fate.
And one day, the world, will see me as great.
Greatness doesn't come, on its own indeed.
But is to be earned, with all your deeds.

So don't feel lonely, if you find yourself alone.
For along with, it brings, the strength to fight & get sown,
Into the hearts of people, who today may frown.
But will be around tomorrow, when you have grown.

RUN

(Thereafter, that day onwards there was no looking back in the life of James. He faced bravely all his hardships, challenged his fate on each & every turn and was moving with pace towards his destiny which he was building with his own hands. But in the process, Tina never returned as she got married to a billionaire and established a name of her own. Then one day, a couple of years after they last met, fate brought them in front of each other. 'RUN' is a detailed version of the emotions that the heart of James is going through at this very instant.)

Walking down the lane,
Saw a girl with fame,
Is she the same?
Or the one with a different name?

Remembered the one,
Together we shared so much fun.
Now that it's done,
I feel to run.

Run away, to the heights of mountains,
Run away, to a place full of fountains.
Runaway, to a place unknown,
Run away, where no one shown.
Run away, is all I feel,
But run away, is not the deal.
Run away, will fill me hate,
All I need, is to just wait.

Prove yourself, and stand up there,
Make a house, she would like to share.
But now that she has come, I don't feel same,
For though she is the one, but with a different name.

PIOUS & PURE; ARE THE WORDS MADE TO JUST LURE

(Today James has reached a point which he always longed for. He now has become a rich & prosperous man with fame. But on his road towards his destiny, James gradually moved closer towards his own self and preferred leading a melancholic life. He no longer sought the company of others. He realized that this world is nothing but a pot of filthy greedy people. For at the time of his need all his relatives who claimed to be his well wishers simply intended to use him for their personal benefits. No one really cared what mattered to him or what he desired. It took a lot for him to finally get himself released out of their clutches. But now that he has acquired fame, all his so called well wishers has flocked him again. Looking at them standing in front of him, his heart hereby makes a satire saying, 'PIOU & PURE; ARE THE WORDS MADE TO JUST LURE'.)

Pious & pure; are the words made to just lure.
Lure the people, who simply fall in trap,
Lure the people who just reside by the map.

Clap, clap, clap is all I could say,
May God provide to those who simply lay.
Fallen are their senses as they are engrossed in play,
Ethics are lost as they do simply say.

Ethics is what I said and I didn't mean morality,
Even that cannot be followed and this is pity.

Where these caretakers lead? I am so unsure,
If only their hearts had been really pure.

All they do is mislead for the sake of their pleasures,
We are the one loosing all our treasures.
It did happen earlier and is happening again,
Are we the fools to become prey for their games?

I stand apart for I did seek true knowledge,
Does it really matter if I didn't complete the college?
Wisdom is what I posses that no college teach,
I have met the height that is beyond their reach.

WILL FOLLOW SOON

(The passionate & aggressive nature of James with passage of time turned ruthless. He no longer cared for anything; all he desired was success, more success and more & more success. He stopped paying heed to the emotions of others. He started manipulating them for his own gains though eventually others too benefited out of it. One night when he was unable to sleep and was trying to relax his mind lying on his terrace wall, he was approached by his soul. 'WILL FOLLOW SOON' is the argumentative conversation that now begins between James and his soul.)

Lying there on the terrace wall,
My soul suddenly gave me a call.
"Though you stand tall, very tall,
How low do you intend to go & fall?"

I listened silently to what the soul said,
May be for I didn't feel going to bed.
Asked the soul, standing near the pole,
"How much more to reach the goal?"

I smiled gently and looked at sky,
Awaiting the moment to bid it goodbye.
"Don't act smart, just answer me why?"
Screamed the soul as its heart cried.

"Ok, my friend", I said as I hugged my soul,
"Your real problem is that you are too pure.

The desire for success has only one cure,
Keep moving ahead at other peoples' lure".

"What more do you desire?" questioned the soul,
I said, "Don't know brother, I just need more.
You do know I intend to regain my innocence,
But the price they ask is too much an expense".

"How can I forget the people that I met?
How can I forget everything that was said?
Go & sleep my brother this world is not for you,
Will follow soon after I send them to zoo".

BLACK OR WHITE

(That night after James had a confrontation with his soul, he was more at ease with his own self. There was some kind of satisfaction that he felt, something that he always knew but never realized. As he did lie on bed, he started to understand things in better perspective and grew stronger. That night when he fall asleep, his heart began singing a song. And the song it's singing now is 'BLACK OR WHITE'.)

I'm a heart, and a heart of knight,
Call me as you please, whether black or white.
I don't care, if it's wrong or right,
All I look, is to win the fight.

Give me love, and take my life,
Try playing games, and I'll cut you by knife.
Playing fair doesn't mean, I don't know the moves,
Just play foul, and find your body by the grove.

I'm wild, and a free spirit,
So be cautious, before getting involved with.
Heart for heart, is all I trade,
All other thoughts, just go get fade.

I can prefer, a pros over maid,
What if she got, a thousand times laid.
For deeds are never, wrong or right,
It's the intention, that ensures categorize.

I don't care, what world terms me,
I lead my life, as I feel it be.
For I'm a heart, and a heart of knight,
So call me as you please, whether black or white.

I RAN SO FAST

(One day sitting alone on the terrace of his villa, James was pondering over his life. More than pondering, it was introspection of his past and his life so far. 'I RAN SO FAST' is a gist of the thoughts that is coming across to him.)

I ran so fast, out of the past,
For the world ahead, looked so vast.
I ran so fast, out of the past,
So that no one could ever spell a cast.

Was I afraid or did I desire?
Of getting burned or to play with fire?

I ran so fast, out of the past,
As if world around me would blow apart.
I ran so fast, out of the past,
For the fear in me, I would end up last.

Did I fear or did I hate?
Of being late or getting devastate?

I ran so fast, out of the past,
I couldn't observe you looking aghast.
I ran so fast, out of the past,
May be I couldn't accept being your option last.

Was it agony or was it enrage?
Of getting laid or to seek revenge?

Now that I stand and look around,
I feel I knew it happened, for it was bound.
Though at times I desire your sound,
I know it's completely futile to turn around.

For I ran so fast, out of the past,
That my end would only be a booming blast.

ON THE MOUNTAIN TOP

(The introspection that James made of his life provided him with a very pleasant feeling, as if it finally brought his disturbed heart to rest. That night he drove to his village. No he doesn't intend to meet someone there. All he wants now is to enjoy the feel of being at the mountain one last time. So here he stands 'ON THE MOUNTAIN TOP' engrossed in his thoughts with a soothing breeze blowing all around.)

Standing above on the mountain top,
I desire the dreams that my heart crops.
Stay close my love around the clock,
And watch my life turn hit with no place for flops.

It's just a phase and will pass out soon,
The day isn't far when everything will bloom.
With you in my arms, I will go high,
And one day we together will fly in sky.

Standing again on the mountain top,
I do stand here in a state of shock.
You are just a lady and no longer love,
For I know my life has become a series of flops.

My love deserted me and is gone forever,
How do you expect me to turn sober?
She was wise and she was clever,
Now I won't loose and I won't loose ever.

Standing once again on the mountain top,
Finally I hit and didn't let my vow flop.
Just watch O lady, for now I will grow,
I will rise high among all you crows.

I have reaped success from dime to dime,
And I have been with women from time to time.
All I need now is all a bit more,
As now my hunger looks to grow.

Standing for the last time on the mountain top,
My hit life seems to me as flop.
Being on the top, with everyone to bow,
Still there's loneliness with no place to go.

Watch out O moon, as I move ahead with flow,
You are the only one that makes my heart glow.
You look so calm, you look so pleased,
So here I come, just give me peace.

DEFINE PURITY, I ASK THE QUESTION AGAIN

Epilogue

(Some of you might be thinking that the way James did end his life was sign of cowardice. But let me remind you that had he been a coward, he would have put an end to his life long back. Whereas he didn't do that, he fought bravely all his life achieving what most mattered to him i.e. accomplishing the promise he once made to Tina, though it was just that at the time of accomplishment Tina wasn't around him to share it the way he desired. He never allowed fate to decide things for him but himself chose & grabbed what he desired; hence as his way was he didn't even allowed fate to decide his end but chose & grabbed it the way he wanted. No, dear friends please don't feel sad for him for people like him don't enjoy pity or sympathy, as they are no cowards but true warriors. Only thing they desire for is love & respect.

'DEFINE PURITY, I ASK THE QUESTION AGAIN', is my salutation to James, along with all those who have in the past or who in present or who will in future lead their life with valour.)

Define purity, I ask the question again,
All my life I have spent seeking the same.
If a virgin person is really so pure,
Where do the one stand, who was cheated by lure?

Purity cannot be measured in terms of moralities,
It's the ethics; that decide the sanctity.
Ethics & moralities in this world are no longer same,
So should we abide by the words of man with fame?

Words are just medium through which they fool around,
Till you get faint and fall on the ground.
It's time we realize what is the variance,
For ethics & moralities posses their difference.

One is applied on the masses, while other belongs to the classes,
Now it's up to you to decide which one deserves the passes.
For one is played with, to ensure sensual living,
While the other is chosen to attain the meaning.

Morality is a universal guidance that can never be achieved,
Ethics belong to individuals who seek them to live.
Live here doesn't mean to just pass the phase,
Those who stand by ethics are worth to be praised.

SECTION - III

EARLY ONE DAY WITH BEAUTIFUL SUNSHINE

Prologue

(Well it's time we get over James and move ahead, so iet me take you to an 'EARLY ONE DAY WITH BEAUTIFUL SUNSHINE'.)

Early one day with beautiful sunshine,
I woke up holding a glass of wine.
Looked across, among the trees of pine,
Saw someone, whom my heart cheered mine.

Moved outside, leaving everything behind,
Searching for the face that caught my mind.
All it took a glance to ensure my heart go blind,
Where is she now? If only I could find.

She appeared from side, coming out of a pond,
Was it simply lust or beginning of a bond?
She walked towards me and asked, "Where are you from?"
All I said was for this day I had grown.

She gave a smile and looked around,
May be she was searching for some place sound.
Well that wasn't the case as I happen to found,
She picked her earring that did fell on ground.

Looking in my eyes, she asked the time,
Then I carefully, chose my line.
Said, "Will you with me forever dine?"
And she walked away saying, "See you at nine".

REJOICE

Prologue

('REJOICE' is look into the feelings of a man, who travelling on a horse, is on his way back to his home from a long voyage. His heart impatiently craves for the moment when he would be back in the arms of his love, unknown of what lies ahead for him.)

Across the hills, the rainbow shines,
Here comes the sound, of thousand chimes.
The birds are whistling, with breeze around,
Hold me my love, in your arms surround

Lying on the ground, with the rains pouring in,
My heart desires, the touch of your skin.
The drops of rain, pressing me gentle,
The clouds above, making my heart go mental.

Come now my love, I need your kiss,
Just as the first one, that carried eternal bliss.
Here I am at your door,
What are you doing lying there on the floor?

My heart longs for you, as it always did,
I'll be with you, even at the cost of highest bid.
What more to pay, than with my life,
If it's the only way, to be together & rejoice.

IN MY HEART FOR ETERNITY

Prologue

('IN MY HEART FOR ETERNITY', is how a man madly in love expressing his feelings before his love, making her aware of all the things he would do to ensure her a beautiful life ahead and at the same time is asking for the permission to hold her hand forever.)

You will reside in my heart for eternity,
And I promise you will never see yourself
immersed in self pity.
I will bestow, entire happiness at your feet,
With all the pleasure, every moment I will greet.
Morning to night, you will stay in my sight,
You like an angel, will always be dressed in white.
I will add colours, beyond imagination in your life,
All I ask for is your nod to be my side.
All your dreams will be enlarged and fulfilled to perfection,
All your desires will be blossomed and quenched
to satisfaction.
Now, as with you in my arms, my body starts to melt,
I hereby declare something I always felt.
Your inclusion in my life, is adding more electrons
to electricity,
You will reside in my heart till the end of eternity.

JUST GIVE ME A CALL

Prologue

('JUST GIVE ME A CALL' is about the bond, the trust, the commitment shared by two hearts in love.)

Just give me a call when you are caught in rains.

I will be there crossing hundreds of mountains,
I will be there crossing thousands of fountains.

Just give me a call whenever you need.

I will come no matter how hard be the deed,
I will come by now that you have sown the seed.

Just give me a call at the hour of despair.

I will come by with an early prepare,
I will come by to ensure the repair.

No, don't give me a call for I will know,
Whether need or desire, the love will still flow.

For, my only love, is you have been,
Will stand by your side during thick or thin.

SECTION -IV

I WILL TAKE YOU THERE

A FAVOUR

Prologue

(Now, let's begin a new story. Raj, a tall, wheatish coloured male with short hairs is an architect by profession. Entered Priya, a free flowing, charismatic interior designer in the life of Raj. Their relation blossomed as they really jelled quite well together. Finally Raj decided to propose and hence he called Priya and asked her to meet him at the park this evening. So as already confirmed, right now he is nervously waiting for Priya to arrive, with the birds humming around all over in the park. And then Priya appears after making him wait for half an hour. And now as he is about to get into the act, he gets filled with fear. The thought that is blocking his mind is no issues, if Priya accepts but what if she tore his heart as paper.Well what follows next? Find out yourself when you turn the page and read 'A FAVOUR')

Time has grown, and so has tide,
I will do or I might.
Here, she comes, and my knees go weak,
Is this the moment or should I wait & seek.

"Don't be afraid", said my heart,
"Unfold your feels, and sing as lark".
I told my heart, "Don't beat so fast,
I'm about, to fulfil the task".

Seeing my state, she gave a smile,
All my words, disappeared by miles.
I gained all courage, and fought all fear,
On the wall, she sat intent to hear.

Down on my knees, I just fall,
With my hands above, I gave her call.
"All I have is just one wish,
You be the water, and I be fish".

Then came the words, I remember still,
What she said made my heart fill.

"I love you now, and will love you forever,
Just for the end, I want a favour".
"Sudden death, is all I need,
Lying in your arms, I ensure my last breathe".

LOVE OF LIFE

(Well, now that Raj & Priya agreed, it just took them six months to call that it was time for wedding bells to ring. It's the wedding day and Raj is excitedly waiting for Priya. There the door opens and enters his 'LOVE OF LIFE'.)

Here she comes walking down the corridor,
A feeling divine, into my heart she bore.
Moving across like a free flowing breeze,
She penetrates my heart, commanding a seize.
Falling on her face, are her hairs so wild,
Boost my tempo, soothingly way mild.
Flows her fragrance, as if perfumes delight,
Envelopes my world, completely with excite.
Her sultry lips with a tinge of red wine,
Oscillates my mind as zephyr plays with chime.
As her moonlit eyes catches my sight,
Even the topsy-turvy world appears to be so right.
She is the one, my love of life,
Without her around, I couldn't have rise.

LOST BOND

(A few years after marriage were pretty smooth, but gradually things started turning a bit rough. It started with petty fights over petty issues, then a shift in priorities. Finally one day they had a big fight and in that fit of rage, Raj stormed out of the house. For hours he stays outside; first in frustration, but later he analyses and now is trying to understand the reasons behind their 'LOST BOND'.)

Those were the days when we flew like doves,
Bond together by the feel of love.
We rocked the world being high & above,
Now why do I doubt, if it really was love?

No matter be the time,
Our hearts always shined.
No matter be the cause,
We used to meet & pause.

No matter be the trouble,
It always got resolved.
No matter be the dispute,
It always got dissolved.

Together we walked and shared the ride,
Together we drove and turned the tide.
We were so close, we were so bright,
Then how could our relation split open wide.

Was it intended or was it destined?
Was it natural or we just played blind?
But now that it happened, I do need to find,
That lost bond, which used to keep us bind.

COME HOME

(Just as Raj realized the blunders made by them, he rushed back home. Reaching home, he ran inside. He searched through the rooms calling her name. But to his utter despair, it was too late for by the time he arrived, Priya had already left. Seeing the sight he just crashed on the floor.

Days, months & years passed but life for Raj just stood still. He searched all over for Priya, but all in vain. Nowadays at times he gets into a very silent depressive state. And if ever he says something, all he says is 'COME HOME'.)

Days are colourless, and the nights are white,
Mornings are empty, and evenings light.
Gone are the days, when they looked bright,
Come home my love, be by my side.

All I need, is a chance once more,
To hold you close, by the shore.
All I need, is a look indeed,
And I know, your heart will greet.

Can't you see my life turn pale?
Can't you see my luck go sail?
Can't you see my heart shed blood?
Finally, me getting drowned in flood.

I agree, it was all my fault,
I was foolish, I was dolt.

I agree I should, have you told,
But things then, weren't in my control.

Come home love, for things we cared,
Come home love, for things we shared.
Come home love, for I love you so,
It's our nest, don't leave it low.

I WILL TAKE YOU THERE

(Exactly twenty years have passed since Raj & Priya fall apart. And also today is their twenty fifth marriage anniversary. Remembering still the old days, he decided to visit the place where he & Priya first met. Getting himself dressed in the suit he worn on the day of their marriage and brushing his hairs though they now have turned white, he finally arrived at the shore. Sitting there at a rock, just as he was looking at the sun going down, he saw a lady. He moved up, walked close to her and stood her side. Together they started looking at the setting sun, holding each others hand. 'I WILL TAKE YOU THERE' presents you with the thoughts that are presently enveloping the mind of Raj while he is looking at the sunset.)

The clock above always ticked my heart,
That how long it's been since we fall apart.
After all these years in isolation,
I remember still our confrontation.

No it wasn't circumstances that turned our foe,
Your shift in priorities enforced our go.
Ya, I didn't compromise for I loved you so,
But you didn't care and left me low.

I simply stormed out of the house,
And returned to find only a mouse.
You walked away out of my life,
Ever since then I have been paying the price.

I lost my balance in utter despair,
Walked along the roads to find if you were near.
Searched all the ways that might lead to you,
All I wanted was yours one last view.

Never did I realize I would be so late,
That all my possessions would be snatched by fate.
Now that I have you found, I can see in your eyes,
That you too have paid a very similar price.

Come with me my love; let's start all over again,
I will take you there, where there is no pain.

YOUR TWINKLING EYES WITH A LOOK DIVINE

Epilogue

(Indeed it was heart warming to see Raj & Priya, get back together. After witnessing the most pleasant sunset of their lives, Raj finally said something to Priya. Well find out, what he did say as he began saying 'YOUR TWINKLING EYES WITH A LOOK DIVINE'.)

Your twinkling eyes,
With a look divine.
Makes my heart,
Go bright, with shine.

Your smile, with a charm
Of thousand roses,
Enlightens my world,
Though despair it posses.

Your fragrance of,
The countryside breeze,
Uplifts my mind,
Beyond the crease.

Your silken touch,
Weakens my knees,
Envelopes my soul,
And brings, me peace.

Life with you, is so nice & pleasant,
Even the past, appears to be so recent.
Be in my arms, forever O Love!
Together we fly, high-high & above.

SECTION - V

ONE NIGHT AT A DISCO

Prologue

(Well, after that soothing sunset with Raj & Priya, let me take you to a thrilling 'ONE NIGHT AT A DISCO'.)

One night at a disco,
I vowed I won't let today turn fiasco.
Moved along brushing bodies divine,
Searched for the one whose eyes did shine.

There she was rocking the floor,
The more I looked, my heart cherished more.
Moved ahead looking straight in her eyes,
I stood up close by her side.

"May I pay you a compliment?" was what I asked,
She replied, "Sure why not, it's no big task".
"Your gaze posses smoothness of a premium scotch", said I with style,
She pondered for a while and finally smiled.

That's how it began and moved up fast,
Now I desire to see this bond last.
Since as she entered, my life turned into a smooth flight,
Exploding my entire plight, for her love is dynamite.

DON'T GO BEAUTY, NOT FOR NOW

Prologue

(No one desires the worst to happen, especially when everything runs smooth and everything seems bright. Still there are a few moments and times when things really aren't under your control. The same is the case with this man who on his way back calls his wife but it turns futile as he comes to know that she has deserted him forever though he kept on repeating 'DON'T GO BEAUTY, NOT FOR NOW'.)

Don't go beauty, not for now,
Not till the moment, I ask you how.

That walk across, the beautiful sand,
Where for the first time, I hold your hand.
The smile on your face, was so pure,
And your excitement was true for sure.

Beautiful still, as you were,
Close to my heart, I find you there.

Though time I proposed, was a bit wrong,
You looked in my eyes, and sang a song.
Thrilled was my life, with you my wife,
Then entered destiny carrying a knife.

I tried hard, to find the cure,
You my love were all so sure.

I told you not, to leave me alone,
But you didn't even receive my phone.

Now hold my hand, and hear my voice,
Wake up my love, and turn the tide.
Don't leave me alone in this city,
Please open your eyes, O my Beauty!

I LIE LOW FOR I FEAR THE TIDE

Prologue

('I LIE LOW FOR I FEAR THE TIDE' is the mindset of a man whom the world called coward but he was quite comfortable with himself. It was only when his love comes to him and says that she feels the same about him that he agrees to explain his mindset.)

I lie low for I fear the tide,
Can't play on flukes, with you my beside.
I lie low for the fear of changes,
Don't know what life ahead arranges.
I lie low for the fear of loss,
Of our bond that today shines with gloss.
I lie low for the fear of fate,
Just don't know what it serves us on plate.
Ya, I do lie low and am not ashamed of it,
For what matters most is how long our hearts click.
I do lie low and ensures a hide,
For I am happy, with you being my side.
The moments we share are so great,
There is no room for Mr. Hate,
But if he interrupts in our life O Mate,
I am not afraid to hold the collar of Fate.

SECTION - VI

GAME

CHEER UP GUYS

Prologue

(Now, it's time for beginning of a new story. So, here comes Alex, a teenaged guy about to enter graduation and who is optimistic, raring to go, raring to explore the world and beholding dreams in his eyes. 'CHEER UP GUYS' is an introduction with Alex & his vibrant personality as he stands in between surrounded by all his friends and says......)

Tall I grew, along with time,
There comes the moment, when all will shine.
Some look gay, some look gloomy,
Cheer up guys, don't act so phoney.

Days gone by, were so sweet,
Days ahead, will still be a treat.
Don't loose heart, for you aren't sure,
Of what comes ahead or what's in store.

Life here was so much fun,
Along with teachers & the nuns.
Life ahead too hope be same,
I'll remember all the names.

Past is gone, and future awaits,
Right here, right now, beyond the gates.
So cherish the past, and look towards future,
Skate along slowly, along the curvature.

Cheer up guys, for this is the moment,
Where life turns, towards development.
So all again, in the name of life,
Let's toast champagne, all tonight.

BELOVED

(The story continues in 'BELOVED', with the emergence of Jenny at the scene whom Alex met at the first day of his college. As, Alex & Jenny moved along, their crush turned into love. So for now enjoy the phase from the point of view of Alex.)

Hold me close and hold me tight,
It's the look in your eyes,
That brings me light.

The way you touch,
The way you hold,
Sublimes my heart & my soul.

It's your fragrance, that drives me crazy,
It's your presence, that makes my world go frenzy.

The moment you stepped, into my world,
You brought me happiness, along with twirl.

I knew, you were my life & my soul,
So never part away,
Or I may loose my goal.

Never in my life, have I been so sure,
Even with passage of time,
Our love will always remain pure.

INSANE

(With the end of graduation ended the love between Alex & Jenny. Why is it that, only after breaking of heart, a person realizes that love is blind? This is the question that nowadays continuously haunts Alex. He always knew that Jenny was a highly ambitious girl, but may be what he never realized was that she would desert him for a rich lad. 'INSANE' is nothing much but a satire, a mock that is being made by Alex, on his own self and on those of his own type.)

Everywhere there is pain,
All I have done is in vain.
My life till now has been without gain,
Can I now call myself insane?

Life was beautiful, life was lovely.
Then came a girl, who was sweet & bubbly.
I gave her love that was gentle & pure.
But all she wanted was just to lure.

She swept my mind, she swept my soul,
And then she left, leaving me in hole.
I asked her once, "What caused your run?"
And then she said, "Darling, its all just fun".

May be in this world, it's wrong to be good,
For then you will be used, just as food.
This is the truth, whether blunt or sharp,
Sooner or later, you are gonna turn warp.

The world around is topsy-turvy,
Nothing here is straight but curvy.
So all my friends, who feel the same,
I think it's time, we call ourselves insane.

REVENGE

(Alex could never get even with himself. May it was because of what Jenny explained to him that he was too good a person and hence not her type. This indeed was a brutal pain. This I call to be brutal pain for it makes your own self stink to you, developing doubts about the goodness in you & the world around. Hence the only thing that came first in the mind of Alex after laughing at self, which he supposed would ultimately bring him peace is 'REVENGE'.)

Go away, and shut the door,
I don't wanna, see you anymore.
I hate you, as I loved O Maid!
Now you go, and get yourself laid.

May be it's all, that you need,
Along with money, fame & greed.
Is this indeed, really your breed?
Or was it just, one of your deeds?

Now that you have, yourself revealed,
You better start, counting beads.
For I am going, to blow you up
Just like a weed, just like a weed.

Wait for the moment, till I get back,
Everything be revenged, and placed back on rack.
I know you will come, for your greed will ensure,
Portraying yourself, still as pure.

This will be, your only mistake.
I'll have the last laugh, though alone to celebrate.

LOVE IN THIS WORLD NO LONGER EXISTS

(Alex gradually moved along though a bit slow at earlier stages but moved up rapidly in the later half. After ten years of passing from the college, he made great strides in his professional life and now is the vice-president of a leading television channel. But even after passage of so many years that pain shows up again from time to time, making him realize that 'LOVE IN THIS WORLD NO LONGER EXISTS'. This evening too, the pain strikes him again as he is sitting inside his royal cabin on the top floor and stares blankly outside the glasses at the white sky.)

Love in this world no longer exists,
Fools are those who try to persist.
Lost are those days when survived the word devotion,
Now it's a battle, a battle of manipulation.

World is just a place, a place filled with crows,
Who cares for bond, a bond that feels to grow?
'Use', use is the word that is in demand,
All other feels just have to face remand.

Right, 'remand' is the game, where everyone blames,
As they fly high, high in their planes.
One that suffers dies in pain,
For he gets burned, burned in flames.

The key to survival, is selecting the game by default,
Overlook others' suffering and replete your vault.
You too will succeed and succeed with flair,
Though love that you desired, will at distance glare.

EMOTION IS DANGEROUS

(In spite of all odds, Alex always led his life with flair and when it comes to moving ahead in the path of life, he possess just one belief i.e. 'EMOTION IS DANGEROUS'.)

Emotion is dangerous; it makes you weak,
Emotion is poisonous; it makes you bleed.
Emotion is a drug; it makes you carve,
Emotion is a shot; finally sinks your heart.

Emotion is contagious; so beware of it,
Emotion is disease; so prepare for it.
Emotion is flu; don't let it stick as glue,
For if it does, you will have no clue.

Let your mind overtake your heart,
Allow no one to pull your happiness apart.
But happiness itself is an emotion,
So what do we do? Is the biggest question

Emotion is lethal; but you need to know how to play,
Mould it the way you want, just like clay.
Use it wisely, for emotion is power,
Look where you stand, on which side of the shower.

Trust your instincts and choose your card,
No matter if you walk all alone on the path.
Work from your mind, but let the heart rule,
And you will emerge winner, in this game of pool.

GAME

(Alex always kept himself too involved in his life & work. All the thoughts of past had diminished. Then as if fate played a game, Jenny made a re-entry into his life. One afternoon she gave him a call and expressed her desire to meet. Though reluctantly at first, Alex finally asked her to meet him at his place by evening. As Alex returned home from his office, he finds Jenny standing there in front of his gate. His first face to face meet with Jenny in more than ten years. Now the question arises, what's next? Just wait & watch as the 'GAME' unfolds.)

Travelling deep, down the lane,
In my memories, you look the same.
You seem still fresh, and red as cherries,
Though you have grown, well into berries.

Since time has flown, fast with fun,
Have you changed, or still carry gun.
Remember the time, when you robbed me first,
All I had, was my heart to serve.

You grabbed it hard, and made me spun,
Even, you got lost, till it got done.
Life since then, has changed a lot,
As you left me, without a thought.

No issues Jenny, then I had no penny,
But now with time, I have got many.

So come on darling, let's go inside,
To celebrate, you being again my side.

Lying on this sofa, I feel relaxed,
Though there was a time, when I preferred your lap.
So my dear Jenny, I think it's time,
You get out, before I count nine.

A PLACE TO LAND

Epilogue

(Finally after settling scores with Jenny, Alex at last felt relieved and refreshed but this state of his didn't last long. As the scars from the past could never get erased and he could never find the peace that he always longed for, but still he found a way through which he moved closer to it. 'A PLACE TO LAND' is the attitude which thereafter he maintained & lived with forever.)

By the sea or by the sand,
My heart desires a place to land.
Flown above the entire hill range,
No one around, completes the maze.

Is she for real or just a dream?
Don't get bluffed by the one with cream.
Here they come, one by one,
Loosing their charm, when it's done.

Mind says, "It's all over".
Heart says, "Just stay, undercover".
Listening to them, all the way through,
Flew along, as I old grew.

Some were brute, some were bright,
Some were cool, and some were nice.

Awaiting still, for the love of life,
Where's the one, of my own choice.

Ha! Who the hell cares, for love of life?
As long I stay, by the sea-side.
That's the way, I do pretend,
Though heart desires a place to land.

SECTION - VII

ONCE UPON A TIME IN A TWILIGHT ZONE

Prologue

(After the tension filled life of Alex, let me present you with a life that we all desire to have. 'ONCE UPON A TIME IN A TWILIGHT ZONE' is all about that desirous life.)

Once upon a time in a twilight zone,
I saw a maiden carrying a cone.
As she came close rang her phone,
And all her surround with the light shone.

It was breezy and a bit damp,
All I wished, if I could prove champ.
As I moved closer, I saw her tears,
Though she looked, to be one without fears.

For that moment the world stood still,
Falling from her wallet, I saw a bill.
Picking it at once, I felt a chill,
Though at the time my heart began to drill.

Pulling up my chances, I called her 'Miss',
Then putting across the bill, said, "I found this".
Suddenly it rained, making us run for shade,
Thanks my Lord, for ensuring this moment made.

We sat at nearby coffee shop and I couldn't ask for more,
My heart announced she was the one for sure.
She smiled at me and she looked so pure,
And I looked into her eyes, with no intentions to lure.

She was so innocent and so divine,
That look in her eyes, boosted my enzymes.
With that twirl in stomach, grew deep my love,
And she became for me above all above.

What to say more, she is my hearts' core,
Wanna know more, ask her for sure.
(Enters wife and says)
"Twenty five years since then, we have been sharing our meals,
Everyday with him is like a sweet dream feel".

LOVING YOU MIGHT HAVE BEEN A SIN

Prologue

('LOVING YOU MIGHT HAVE BEEN A SIN' is a beautiful note being presented by a guy to his love after she calls that it's all over.)

Loving you might have been a sin,
I do breathe you as a fish does with her fins.
But now that you have pinched my heart with pin,
My heart is left stranded in a bin.

All I desired was forever see you grin,
Though your hate has now crossed the brim.
Once we said, no matter be the odds we are always in,
Now how can you alone decide to make our love trim?

Submerged myself in your love I have,
Drown me now or have me save.
There was a time when you really were brave,
Now that you switch; my heart turns rave.

No I desire not any of your pity,
You need it more, though you pretend to act witty.
I can see your beneath; there is love, no hate,
What more can I say, now that you have chosen fate.

I will move ahead, though your memories would remain,
Will lead my life though partly in pain.
But you my love, will find no serenity,
For your life would turn a portrayal of self pity.

NO I DON'T FEEL ANY SHAME

Prologue

(Love is a feeling, a bond between two hearts. When you love, you love the person irrespective of their trade. For it has nothing to do with past of an individual, it's all about the authenticity in commitment between those hearts for their present and towards their future. 'NO I DON'T FEEL ANY SHAME' is a declaration of a man who is in love with an ex-prostitute.)

No I don't feel any shame when I call your name,
You live in a world that is insane.
It's not you they disgrace; they disgrace their own self,
Right that's where I faulted, for they have turned to elf.

Hadn't they, they wouldn't have seen you like that,
With the eyes of wolf, just intending to catch.
You no longer categorize in their match,
You belong to a zone that is above their patch.

You may be called by the name of prostitute,
But you are the one who laid foundations of their institute.
Who cares for them or to what they say?
You are forever mine, no matter what come may.

You are the one that guides this world,
You are the one that shows the meaning of love.

Not with money or picture of doves can they find,
A love that ensures the hearts' eternal bind.

YA, I KNOW I DON'T SING YOUR PRAISES

Prologue

('YA, I KNOW I DON'T SING YOUR PRAISES', is the summary of reasons that are being forwarded by a pessimist man who is in love but feels afraid to express it.)

Ya, know I don't sing your praises,
Though I do enjoy coming up with phrases.
Ya, I know I don't admire your dreamy eyes,
Though they bring me hope & delight.
Ya, I know I don't ask for your magical touch,
Even when it soothes me with solace needed much.
Ya, I know I don't linger around always,
In spite craving for it, n number of days.
Ya, I know I don't call you often,
Though just by your voice, my enraged mood softens.
Ya, I know I don't bring you presents,
Though I labour for it, just as a peasant.
Ya, I know I do enjoy to tease,
But don't you ever take, me wrong please.
It's not that I don't love your face,
It's just that, I prefer playing safe.

Section - VIII

No Matter What It Takes

I NEVER MEANT TO BREAK YOUR HEART

Prologue

(Rahul & Jia were two love birds happily married together. Rahul worked with a multinational company while Jia was a housewife. As planned by some evil minds, those who intended to see Rahul fall, he gets framed with a girl. On becoming aware of the case, he runs to clear things with his wife. But before he could it was too late, for till then she got blinded by the presence of false proofs. Now standing in front of his flat Rahul pleads for a hearing and continuously knocks the door but Jia just refuses to hear or to open. 'I NEVER MEANT TO BREAK YOUR HEART', is what Rahul says before leaving away.)

I never meant to break your heart,
I never meant to pull your soul apart.
I never desired us to depart,
I never desired you to shut your heart.
It's the place I really reside,
An exit from there would cause my demise.
I am now left with no other choice,
I am willing to pay the final price.
I will fight till my last breath,
Even though it ends with me being wretch.
The pain caused by this stain,
Cannot get washed in the rains.

No, I will not die of shame,
I will again prove to be the same.
Just don't let dubiety takeover your belief,
For it's my strength and my only relief.
Do wait O Love, for you have been my foresight,
Will be back soon, proving self pure as white.

THE SUN IS GOING DOWN AND SO IS MY HEART

(A few days later, came the news that Jia did finally leave the city with no one being sure where she left for and with it got broke the only thread of confidence that was left in Rahul. Dejectedly he walks back to his home, enters inside and sits on the terrace floor. 'THE SUN IS GOING DOWN AND SO IS MY HEART', is the emotional state he is experiencing at this moment.)

The sun is going down,
And so is my heart.
What's about these sunsets?
That gets them called art.

Is it for their colour?
That gives us peace.
Or is there something else?
That's hidden behind the trees.

Calls me my love,
Or is it mere illusion?
If only our hearts,
Had made successful fusion.

Things got replaced,
Such as love with hate.

If only you could understand,
O dear, my mate!

The time we shared,
Was bright & so great.
All I asked,
Was if you could wait.

May be it was destined,
Or may be it was fate.
The love between us,
Will shine though late.

Your love like this sunset,
Gave me all the peace.
One day, I'll be back,
Asking your hand, on my knees.

CHERISHED DESIRE

(Even after moving away from Rahul, the heart of Jia declines to stop forget him. No matter how much she tries to assure herself, her heart simply refuses to accept the factuality. 'CHERISHED DESIRE', is a realization cum dream that Jia is coming across as she stands near an open window, looking outside engrossed in her thoughts.)

The breezing air, is making me feel fly,
The thunderous rain, filling my heart with joy.

Looking, at a beautiful rose,
Makes me, feel shy,
While when presented with a bunch of it,
My heart says, "Hi".

Comes a voice,
That calls my name.
And I sense,
If the voice is same.

I start looking around,
To find no one there.
But only a smile,
On my face to share.

There comes the voice again,
And strikes, my mind, heart & soul, all at the same.

Standing before me,
Is my love of life, in circumstances bizarre.
To be in his arms, forever,
Is my only desire.

NO MATTER WHAT IT TAKES

(One day Rahul received some news about the whereabouts of Jia. Along with he also heard that she is severely ill. He travelled all the way across and finally reached the hospital where Jia was admitted. But on reaching there what he came to know shattered his soul completely, as his heart begins to say, 'NO MATTER WHAT IT TAKES'.)

No matter, what it takes,
We agreed, we would make.
Keeping, everything at stake,
A bond, that would never shake.

True were the words,
And true were intents.
But the views of our fate,
Were quite different.

Together we fought, and we fought hard,
Without realising what laid on cards.
Then came the cruel time, wearing a dress of brass,
And she passed away, lying there on the grass.

She left away, and I was left behind,
Along went our dream, to be together & unite.
Time changes things, but not thought that posses wings,
I still see her around, and that's love with no bounds.

It's the game, played by our fate,
We stay on, either sides of the gate.
Like, the sun & the moon or day & night,
We stay in sight, but can't unite.

MOON SHINES BRIGHT AMIDST THE CLOUDS

Epilogue

(Seeing the final departure of his love, thereafter Rahul lost all his mental stability. He simply kept on wandering places and often when 'THE MOON SHINES BRIGHT AMIDST THE CLOUDS', he usually stands above that hill and confronts his destiny & the destiny maker again & again and night after night.)

Moon shines bright amidst the clouds,
But my mind is filled with doubts.
Looking above at the stars high,
Only question my heart asks; 'Why?'

Why does time runs so fast?
Why did we have to fell apart?
Why do we live on different sides of world?
Why did our lives take a curl?

Neither was I wrong and nor were you,
Then why did it happen in spite our love being true?
If this is what they call fate,
Then it's the only thing, I most hate.

Answer me now O my Lord, O Great!
Why did you snatch my love, my mate?

You took me high, you made me fall,
Is this justice what you call?

Why my Lord, you love to play,
Assuming us to be made of clay?
Answer me O Lord! Answer me now,
How could you do this? Tell me, how?

I need no mercy, I need no pity,
I know how to survive, all alone in the city.
Spare me O Lord! I don't need more favours,
Just watch out if someday you taste your own flavours.

SECTION - IX

I AGREE

Prologue

('I AGREE' is the way a very practical man is hereby approaching his most desired love prospect.)

I agree to share my love,
I agree to stand above.
I agree to fulfil your dreams,
I agree to accept you as beauty queen.

I agree to be by your side,
I agree to be there, whether day or night.
I agree to make you smile life long,
I agree to sing when you desire a song.

I agree never, to be rude,
I agree never, to act brute.
I agree never, to say lie,
I agree never, to make you cry.

I agree to give you love of life,
I agree to ensure you always rejoice.
I agree to love you more than you think,
I agree to keep you always in pink.

I agree to stand by all my commitments,
But before that, you need to sign an agreement.

I hereby decline to love you more,
Let me complete before you rush to shore.

Look I am shrewd and I am mean,
What I am saying is not unseen.
If I give love, I do expect more,
So sign the agreement, if you are sure.

WAITING STILL

Prologue

(We all know that destiny has its own way of playing games with us. 'WAITING STILL' is also a game played by destiny on this man who is eagerly waiting for his date to arrive back.)

Waiting still down the lane,
I look around people, with no gain.
Searching for the one with the eyes blue,
Just don't know which way she flew.

Moving close towards the adjacent tower,
I wait still next to a flower.
It's been so long since she left,
Should now I report; my hearts' theft.

I can sense, her being here,
Just don't know, she is where.
Waiting still for her to come,
I tumbled over a big thrash drum.

Waiting still for so long,
I don't understand, what's been wrong.
Came a call and I answered my cell,
With what I heard, my heart fell.

Why did she turn suddenly unfair?
To find true love, is really so rare.

It's since been raining, but I don't care,
Walking through the time, is a formality mere.

Waiting still to catch my last flight,
My heart finally, agrees to cease the fight.
Waiting still for us to unite,
Here I stand, by her death beds' side.

MY HEART CRIES AND WEEPS ALL ALONE

Prologue

(Well 'MY HEART CRIES AND WEEPS ALL ALONE' is again an agony of a man who has been denied the company of his love by fate. Hereby he pours his heart out, though in a different way.)

My heart cries and weeps all alone,
Gone are the days when the sun shone.
Am I the same or am I a clone?
All my happiness has apart been blown.

You blossomed my life as the season spring,
Now I am left alone, to fight in the ring.
All I asked for, is to feel you breath again,
All I asked for is the feel when dry land meets rain.

I am left alone to face this game of ball,
Just as autumn, makes the leaves fall.
All I asked for, is to feel again shade of your hairs,
All I asked for is the feel when a child enters fair.

Alone I am left, completely tired & torn,
Similar when summer dries the river or pond.
All I ask for, is to feel again depth of your eyes,
All I ask is the feel when a man happily dies.

Don't leave me alone, in this weather,
Act as winter and provide me leather.
Just as it covers, entire ground with snow,
Take me along, to the world with glow.

I FEEL

Prologue

('I FEEL' is the collection of the experiences and the most precious moments of the life of this lucky satisfied old soul.)

I feel it all my surround,
I feel its passionate mystic bounce.
With your love all around,
I lie peacefully on this ground.

Though it happened all so brisk,
I still remember our first ever kiss.
It was the moment of my life O Miss,
When we shared divine eternal bliss.

The taste of your lips still lingers on,
Even after thousands of sunsets gone.
I feel it still deep inside sown,
Though with time, it has only grown.

The beauty of the night,
When I first hold you tight.
All that happened,
After we shared a big fight.

Fresh in my memory still, softness of your hand,
That made me feel, as water drains sand.

I flew high above, I wasn't on land,
The love we shared was so royal and so grand.

Then came the day when you bid me goodbye,
All I could feel was only to cry.
You looked with your easing eyes and asked me why,
And I said thanks for being only my.

I feel it still, all my around,
I still feel its passionate mystic bounce.
With your love still all around,
Finally I lie peacefully in this ground.

IT'S NOT FAIR TO STAND & STARE

Prologue

(Now, forgetting everything let's talk about two lovers, who have been acclaimed & renowned for ages for their divine & eternal bond. You wanna know their names, I will surely tell you that but let's first hear what one says to another, as he begins with 'IT'S NOT FAIR TO STAND & STARE'.)

It's not fair, to stand & stare,
You being far, and me left here.
You are the one, rare, who is,
But I am the one, without deceit.

Thousand of admirers, you may have,
None like me, is the only fact.
Time & tide, changes the looks,
But I am the one, who loves you, by books.

Above you stand, shining bright,
illuminating hearts, with your light.
Though you shine, you stay alone,
Do you find love, a one-sided zone?

O dear Moon! Don't you, feel sad,
Me too alone, but still I am glad.
Apart we are, but together we stand,
There is no need, to just pretend.

In your company, I feel delight,
Be there always, in my sight.
I dark earth, and you moon white,
I give you love, and you give me light.

LIE BY SWORD

Prologue

(All my friends who desire love but feel may be it's not for them; just relax. Here I present, 'LIE BY SWORD', which is feeling of a man who too cherishes love, but at the same time realizes that may be love is not in his destiny. No matter if he is in love or not, still just the thought of love is the thing that keeps him alive and is his drive. So do remember his words and keep driving your life with enthusiasm.)

Take my breath, take my life,
But do my Lord; give me love that's nice.

Life though, is all a treat,
But life still, is incomplete.
Been along, with a lot of faces,
But not the one, that was on top of aces.

What do you need, from me O Lord!
I just did, as you have taught.
Don't you think, that I deserve,
A love that's sweet, and to preserve.

Life so long, has been through battles,
When do I get, time to raise cattle?
Don't tell me, that's all you got,
Just for this, all along I fought.

Please O Lord! Hear my voice,
Else, I go mad, and no more be wise.
You don't care, you love play dice,
Hence my Lord, it's time I rise.

Now that I know, it's all about choice,
Sure my Lord, enjoy your game of dice.
My path is sure, no more to lure,
I know my end, and that's the cure.

For, I have fought hard, all the way,
And I have fought brave, till today.
So that's the way, O mighty Lord!
I lie in the grave, by my sword.

MY LITTLE SISTER

Prologue

(Love is a strange feeling. A feeling where you strive to see a smile on the face of the person you love. And that particular smile on that particular face is all that matters at that hour of time. As it brings us a unique pleasure & satisfaction, which no worldly matter can bring.

Now that's how I feel in the company of my little sister. And hence last but not the least, here comes a sweet poem dedicated to my sweet sister by the name 'MY LITTLE SISTER'.)

My little sister,
She is a miss, and not a mister.

Cute is her smile,
Takes my breath, away for a while.
Charming is her way,
From morning, till the end of day.

Beautiful are her eyes,
They make her look wise.
Lucky are her feet,
They make your dream come meet.

She is my heart, she is my soul,
To see her happy, is my only goal.

She loves to dance, she loves to sing,
Every time the music says ding-ding-ding.

She is, the best of all,
And her name is 'ANGEL', as we call.